Contents

Teachers' notes	1	Parrot counting cards	17
Twenty faces	5	Counting cards and times tables	18
Animals	6	Peanuts	19
More animals	7	Seeds	20
0 to 20 number cards	8	Seed sums	21
Bus counting cards	9	Check your handwriting	22
Up and downstairs	10	Writing practice: 2s and 3s	23
On and off	11	4s and 5s	24
Bus sums 1	12	6s, 8s and 9s	25
Bus sums 2	13	Lots of legs 1	26
Dotty dragon	14	Lots of legs 2	27
Fruit	15	Caterpillars	28
Tins	15	Frogs	29
Dotty parrot	16	Legs to twenty	30 to 32

Teachers' notes

Aim of this book
The aim of this book is to provide you with well-presented and mathematically valuable supplementary material which will link with your existing scheme of work for mathematics, and which children will enjoy using. To help you make the best use of the activities, please read the following notes.

Printing
Although photocopying on to white paper may be the simplest way for you to copy the activities in this book, do consider other alternatives. Some pages benefit from copying directly on to card; some look much more interesting when printed on coloured paper or card. If your school does not have the facilities to do this, you may be able to have copies made using a duplicator or printing machine at a larger primary school or secondary school close to you, or perhaps at a teachers' centre.

To keep reusable cards or worksheets in good condition, put them inside plastic wallets, laminate them, or cover them with clear sticky plastic. Even copies made on paper, not card, are surprisingly strong when covered.

Record keeping and storage
We have not provided a separate system of record keeping for these activities, as most teachers prefer to add to their existing scheme of records. You could use the child's own maths writing book to make a note of activities used, when this would be helpful information to have. Worksheets can usually be fastened into the child's book using a piece of sticky tape at the side, like an extra page in the book, to act as a reminder of an activity completed.

Mathematical content
This book provides activities to help children with counting, reading and writing numbers, and using addition, subtraction, multiplication and division in context. Written work is linked to practical activity, and children are given the opportunity to make up questions and problems for each other. Children are encouraged to use calculators, as the calculator provides a strong motive for children to learn and use the symbols +, −, x, ÷ and =, and to make sure, for example, that fourteen is entered as 14, not 41.

Every activity needs introducing by the teacher if children are to make the most of it; a few moments spent discussing their work once children have finished are also obviously worthwhile. Sometimes, activities may be taken home to talk about with parents or other family members.

Although the title of this book is *Numbers to 20* you will find that as children grow in confidence they will extend many of the activities to use larger numbers.

◆ ESSENTIALS FOR MATHS: Numbers to 20

Notes on individual activities

Page 5: Twenty faces

A simple counting activity. Some children may realise that their totals of happy and sad faces should come to 20.

Pages 6 and 7: Animals and more animals

These two sheets make a line of 14 animals under flaps, so that you can count forwards (none, 2, 4, 6, 8, 10, 12, 14) and backwards, as well as lifting flaps more randomly and counting up how many animals you can see altogether. Glue works better than sticky tape for fixing the two sheets together, as it is easier to fold.

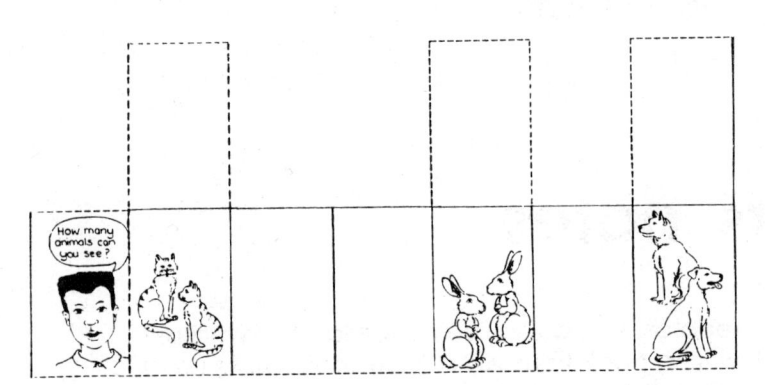

Page 8: 0 to 20 number cards

Print this page on card, using different colours if you want to make more than one set, to make it easier to sort them out. You will probably think of several ways in which you can use them, but here are a few suggestions:
- **Putting them in order:** shuffle the cards. Can the child lay them out in order, smallest to largest, or vice versa? Just use the 0 to 15 cards at first, then 0 to 20.
- **Give me a clue:** this is a game for two people. Shuffle the cards and share them between you. When it is your turn, choose one of your cards and give your friend a clue about it. For example, if your number is 18, you could say 'It is 2 bigger than 16'. If your friend gets it right, she wins the card. Then she gives you a clue for one of her numbers.
- The number cards can also be used with the Bus and the Parrot counting cards.

Pages 9 to 13: Buses

The bus counting cards provide a simple but very effective way of practising counting and simple sums in an easy to understand context. This is how to make one set of the equipment:
- Make 4 copies of page 9 on card, to make 8 bus cards. Alternatively, print copies on paper and then mount them on card.
- Colour the buses. Leave the windows plain.
- Trim each card to fit a suitable storage box (for example, a 2-litre ice-cream tub or a large sandwich box). Cover each card with clear sticky plastic. Label the box.
- Make 'people' to count from dried butter beans marked with a permanent pen (about 15 to 20 per card). You can have black people as well as white by using brown spray paint. Lay the beans on a sheet of newspaper; spray one side and leave to dry. Then turn them over, spray that side, and leave to dry. Draw on faces with your permanent pen.
- Make copies of page 9 on paper, trim off the top and bottom of the pages along the dotted lines, and cut along the centre to make separate lorry sheets. Do not trim off the left-hand side. Children can use these sheets for their own recording; they may like to staple several sheets together to make a 'Bus Book'.

Once children are familiar with the counting cards, they can usually work without adult help for quite a while, but you need to work with them at first. The activities are all meant for two children working together. To begin with, concentrate on counting, adding and taking away. Here are a few ideas:

- **Free play**
Children will concentrate better when introduced to more directed activities if they have had some time to play with the cards and counters before you start.

- **Counting**
First, decide on a number to practise. You could do this by choosing a card from the number cards (see page 8), or simply by letting the children choose. Each child should have four bus cards and he or she should put the 'practice number' of people on each bus. Finally, they can each check their friend's four cards, and then choose a new number to practise.

- **Simple sums**
Make up some sums for each other and use the buses and people to work the sums out. For example, 'There were seven people on the bus and eight more got on. How many people were on the bus now, altogether?' or 'Fourteen

◆ ESSENTIALS FOR MATHS: Numbers to 20

people were on the bus, then five got off. How many people were still on the bus?'

• **Sums with a calculator**
Use a calculator to check your sums and to help children see the importance of the symbols +, – and =. Make up a sum like the ones above. One child uses the buses and people to work it out, whilst the other child does it on a calculator, and both children try the sum in their heads, too. Swap the calculator and the equipment with each other for the next sum.

NB Another book in this series, Numbers to 9, includes a useful workcard which provides suggestions for using the counting cards in an illustrated A5 format, to keep in the storage box with each set of equipment. Numbers to 9 also provides two sets of counting cards, Elephants and Lorries, which can be used in the same way as Buses and the set provided later in this book, Parrots (see pages 17 to 21).

Pages 10 to 13 provide further linked work. Children may benefit from using several copies of pages 10, 11 and 13, or your may want them to use plain paper to make up their own pictorial sums.

Pages 14 and 16: Dotty dragon and dotty parrot

Dot-to-dots are a good way to practise recognising numerals in order, in this case from 0 to 20. Make sure children realise they should join the dots, not the numbers. Try working backwards, joining the dots from 20 down to 0, too.

Page 15: Fruit and Tins

This page makes two A5 worksheets, one totalling 15 objects and the other 20. Children can make up another sheet of their own in the same format, to try on a friend.

Pages 17 to 21: Parrots

The Parrot counting cards are used in a similar way to the Bus counting cards (see pages 9 to 13). Please read the instructions for making the cards given in the notes above.

Use sunflower seeds as the 'counters' for these cards. They can be bought from a pet shop fairly cheaply. The black-and-white sunflower seeds are more attractive to use than the brown ones.

Print page 18 back-to-back with itself to make two A5 copies of notes about using the counting cards to establish times tables facts, initially up to 20, but extending to higher totals as the child gains in confidence. Keep a copy of the notes in each box of equipment as a reminder to adults or older children who are helping by giving extra practice at home or in school.

Pages 22 to 25: Writing practice

Print page 22 on card and cover it for longer life. Provide the children with rough paper and some large counters, and show them how to check the way they write one number. Encourage them to check the others, either on their own or with a friend. Emphasise two things: they way they form the numeral and the final appearance of the number.

Many children find it helpful if you (or themselves) write out a reminder of the numbers they should practise, for example, 'I need to practise writing 2, 3, 5 and 8. This week I will concentrate on 2 and 3. I will check again on Friday.'

Writing practice is most effective in short frequent sessions. Provide the 'Check' card so that the child can look at the numerals with arrows. There are many ways of organising the practice; one way is to write the two or three numbers which a child is concentrating on, two or three times each on a blank dice. The child throws the dice, then has to write that number as carefully as possible.

Pages 23, 24 and 25 each provide further practice, and can each be used more than once if wished.

Pages 26 and 27: Lots of legs 1 and 2

These pages provide illustrations of multiplication. Many children find it helpful to count the animals' legs on the drawings, as well as adding up in their heads and trying the sum on a calculator. Encourage them to say both '8 lots of 2 is 16' and '8 times 2 equals 16'; children benefit from realising from an early stage that there are usually several ways of expressing each mathematical statement. Once a child has completed page 26 successfully, they can use copies of page 27, either individually or working with friends to make up puzzles for each other.

Page 28: Caterpillars

A number story which provides a reason for needing to know a total!

Page 29: Frogs

This sheet concentrates on multiples of 4, in order: 4, 8, 16, 20 or 20, 16, 8, 4. Print copies on paper which is reasonably thick (80g or 90g) and do not

◆ ESSENTIALS FOR MATHS: Numbers to 20

let children use felt-tipped pens for their colouring, otherwise the frogs will show through to the back of the paper rather than being hidden when you have folded it up.

Pages 30 to 32: Legs to 20

A game to practise totals to 20.

Print copies on card and cut out the twenty playing cards and the instruction strip (the left-hand side of page 30). Score along the lines on the instructions, then fold in a zigzag to the same size as a card; the set can then be stored neatly, with the title of the game on top and an elastic band around it. Make sure that children know how many legs each creature has before they start to play; the caterpillar has 16, spider has 8, beetle has 6, frog 4, bird 2 and fish none.

With twenty cards, the game is best for two players. Make two copies, i.e. forty cards, for three or four players.

National Curriculum: Maths

In addition to the relevant programmes of study in AT1, the following PoS from AT2 are relevant to the activities in this book:

Level 1
- counting, reading, writing and ordering numbers to at least 10.
- learning that the size of a set is given by the last number in the count.
- understanding the language associated with number, e.g., 'more', 'fewer', 'the same'.
- understanding the conservation of number.
- making a sensible estimate of a number of objects up to 10.
- using addition and subtraction, with numbers no greater than 10, in the context of real objects.

Level 2
- knowing and using addition and subtraction facts up to 10.
- solving whole-number problems involving addition and subtraction.
- comparing two numbers to find the difference.

Level 3
- learning and using addition and subtraction facts to 20 (including zero).
- learning and using multiplication facts up to 5 × 5.

Scottish 5–14 Curriculum: Mathematics

Attainment outcome	Strand	Attainment targets	Level
Number, money and measurement	Range and type of number	Work with whole numbers 0 to 20 (count, order, read/write statements, display on calculator).	A
	Add and subtract	Add and subtract mentally for numbers 0 to 10.	A
		Add and subtract mentally for numbers 0 to 20; in some cases beyond 20.	B
	Multiply and divide	Multiply and divide mentally by 2, 3, 4, 5, 10 within the confines of these tables.	B
Information handling	Collect	Obtain information for a task from a picture.	A
	Organise	Count, sort into specific sets.	A
	Display	Use pictures.	A
	Interpret	From displays by locating and counting.	A

Scottish Attainment Target chart compiled by Margaret Scott and Susan Gow

◆ Name _____

Twenty faces

◆ Draw the children's faces. Make some happy and some sad.

◆ How many children look happy? _____

◆ How many look sad? _____

◆ ESSENTIALS FOR MATHS: Numbers to 20

◆ Name _____

Animals

◆ Colour in the animals. Cut along the dotted lines to the middle of the page.

fold along here

Cut this section out completely.

How many animals can you see?

◆ ESSENTIALS FOR MATHS: Numbers to 20

◆ Name _____

More animals

◆ Colour in the animals. Glue the bottom of this sheet under the top line of page 6 to make fourteen animals in a row.

fold along here

◆ ESSENTIALS FOR MATHS: Numbers to 20   7

0 to 20 number cards

◆ Make sure that the dark band is along the bottom of each card when you cut them out.

0

1	2	3	4	5
6	7	8	9	10
11	12	13	14	15
16	17	18	19	20

◆ ESSENTIALS FOR MATHS: Numbers to 20

Bus counting cards

◆ ESSENTIALS FOR MATHS: Numbers to 20

◆ Name _____

Up and downstairs

◆ Draw some people on each bus.

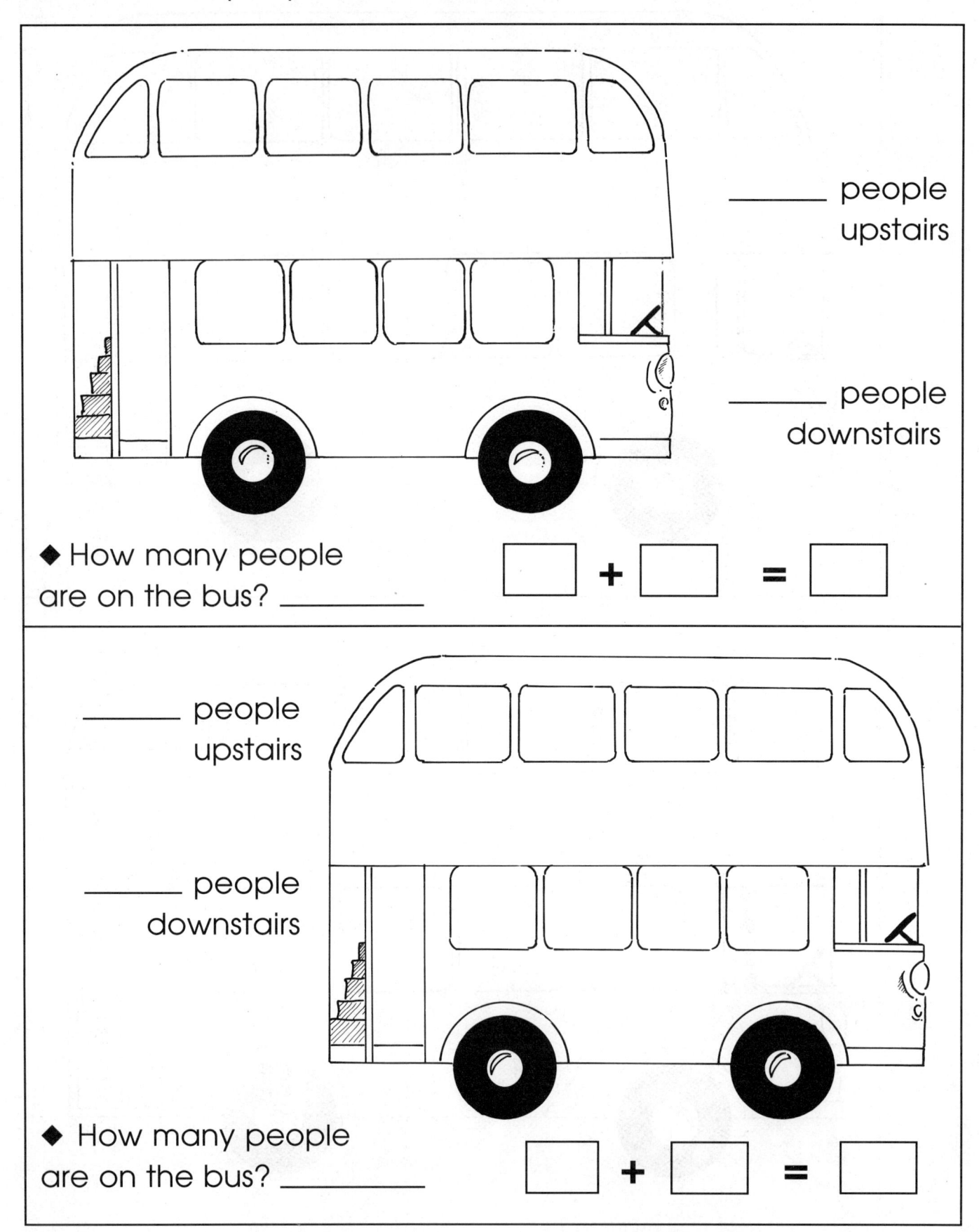

_____ people upstairs

_____ people downstairs

◆ How many people are on the bus? _____

☐ + ☐ = ☐

_____ people upstairs

_____ people downstairs

◆ How many people are on the bus? _____

☐ + ☐ = ☐

◆ Name _____

On and off

◆ Make up your own sums. Draw the pictures.

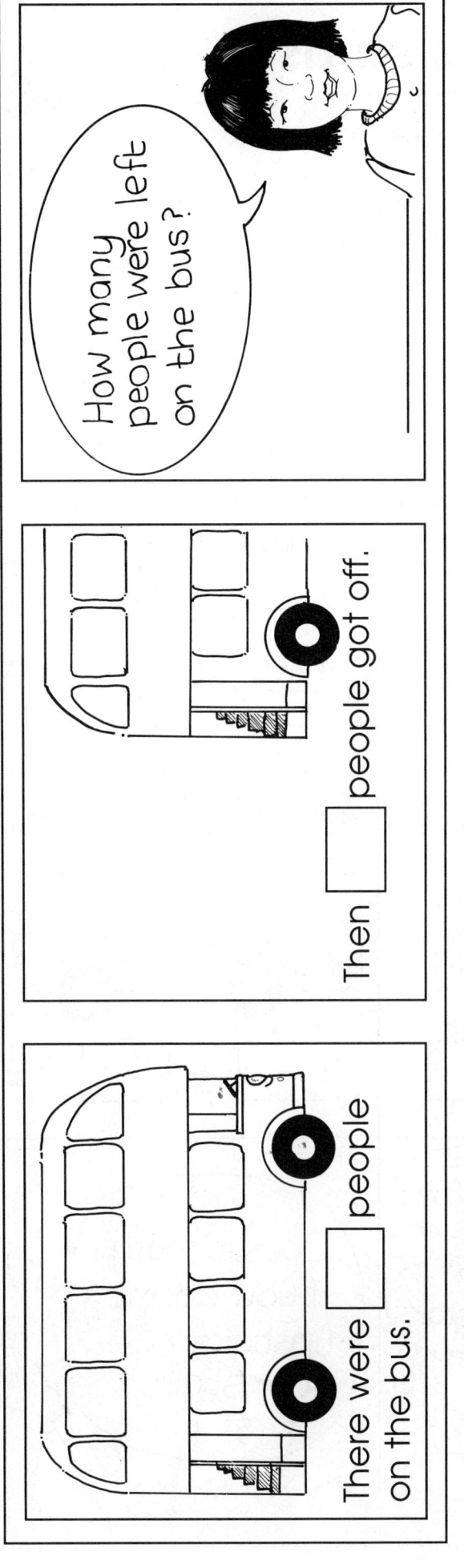

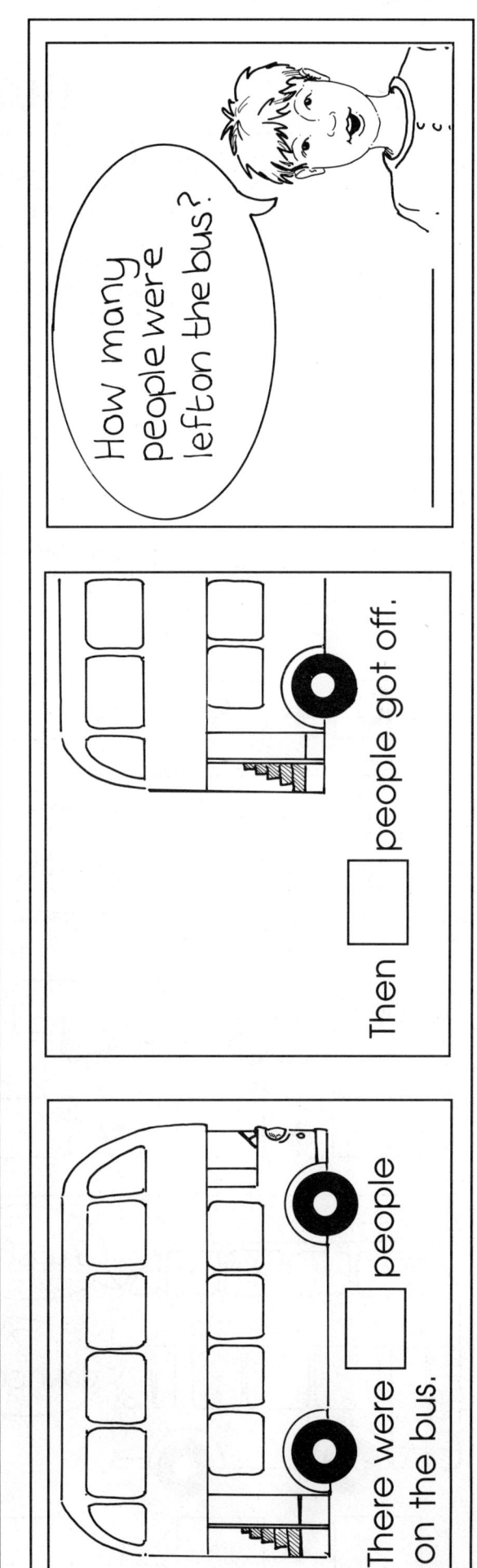

There were ☐ people on the bus.

Then ☐ people got off.

How many people were left on the bus? _____

There were ☐ people on the bus.

Then ☐ people got off.

How many people were left on the bus? _____

◆ ESSENTIALS FOR MATHS: Numbers to 20

◆ Name _____

Bus sums 1

How many people are on these buses? Use the bus counting cards to help you, if you want to.

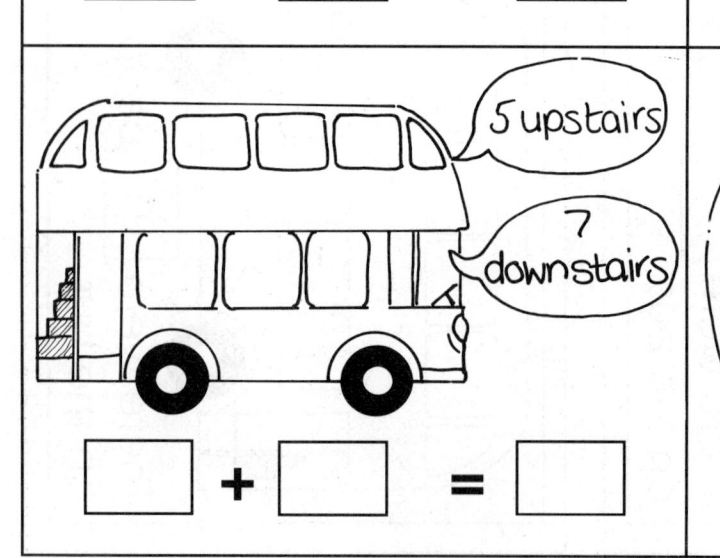

---

10 upstairs
4 downstairs

| 10 | + | 4 | = | |

---

6 upstairs
3 downstairs

| | + | | = | |

---

7 upstairs
8 downstairs

| | + | | = | |

---

11 upstairs
3 downstairs

| | + | | = | |

---

5 upstairs
7 downstairs

| | + | | = | |

Does it matter if you count upstairs or downstairs first?

◆ ESSENTIALS FOR MATHS: Numbers to 20

◆ Name _____

Bus sums 2

These sums are for

Make up some sums. Give them to your friend to try.

_____

___ upstairs	___ upstairs
___ downstairs	___ downstairs
☐ + ☐ = ☐	☐ + ☐ = ☐

___ upstairs	___ upstairs
___ downstairs	___ downstairs
☐ + ☐ = ☐	☐ + ☐ = ☐

___ upstairs	___ upstairs
___ downstairs	___ downstairs
☐ + ☐ = ☐	☐ + ☐ = ☐

◆ ESSENTIALS FOR MATHS: Numbers to 20

◆ Name _____

Dotty dragon

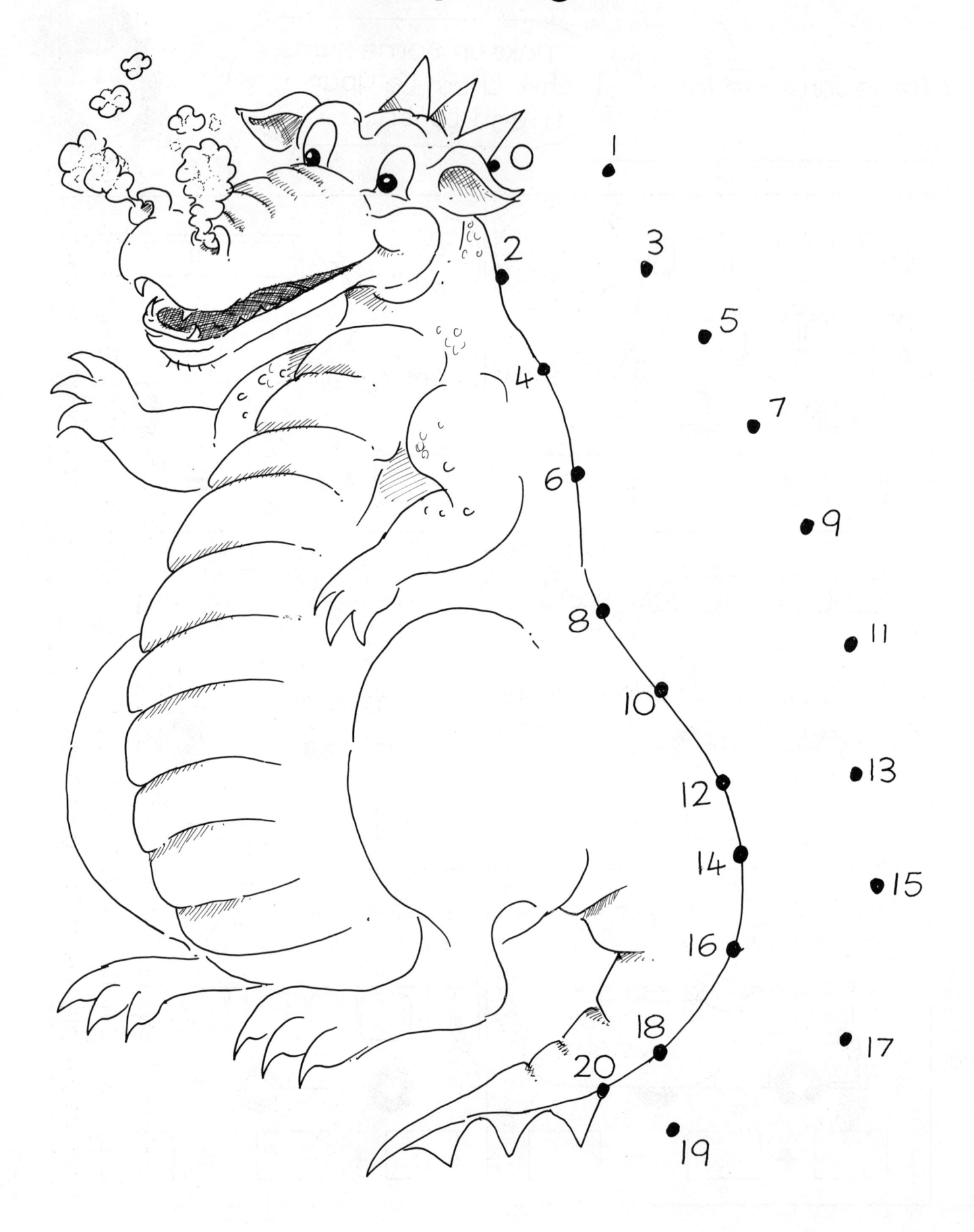

◆ ESSENTIALS FOR MATHS: Numbers to 20

◆ Name _____

Tins

"Do you like baked beans or sweetcorn the best?"

◆ Colour them in.

How many tins of beans are there? _____
How many tins of sweetcorn? _____
How many tins altogether? _____

◆ Name _____

Fruit

"Do you like apples or bananas the best?"

◆ Colour them in.

How many apples are there? _____
How many bananas are there? _____
How many pieces of fruit altogether? _____

◆ ESSENTIALS FOR MATHS: Numbers to 20

◆ Name _____

Dotty parrot

◆ ESSENTIALS FOR MATHS: Numbers to 20

Parrot counting cards

ESSENTIALS FOR MATHS: Numbers to 20

Counting cards and times tables

Notes for parents and teachers

Counting cards provide a practical context to help children see the connection between repeated addition and multiplication.

The example used here is the 'Parrots' set, but the same activities can be done with other sets of counting cards.

The activities are all intended for two children working together.

Suppose you want to learn your 3 times table. Take it in turns to ask each other a question and check each other's answers. Here are a few ideas:

Three seeds each
Choose how many parrots to use.

> There were ☐ parrots.
> They had three seeds each.
> How many seeds was that altogether?

Use the parrot cards and seeds to help you work out the answers.

Three parrots
Decide how many seeds to give them.

> I've got three parrots.
> I want to give them ☐ seeds each.
> How many seeds do I need?

Sharing seeds between three
Use the 0 to 20 number cards and three parrot cards.
- Choose a number card. Count out that number of seeds.
- How many seeds can each parrot have? And how many seeds are left over, if any?

Using calculators
Use number cards from 0 to 7 and three parrot cards.
- Choose a number card. Count out that number of seeds for each parrot. How many seeds have you got altogether?
- Check with a calculator. You can do it in two ways.

Suppose you gave each parrot ☐ 5 seeds:

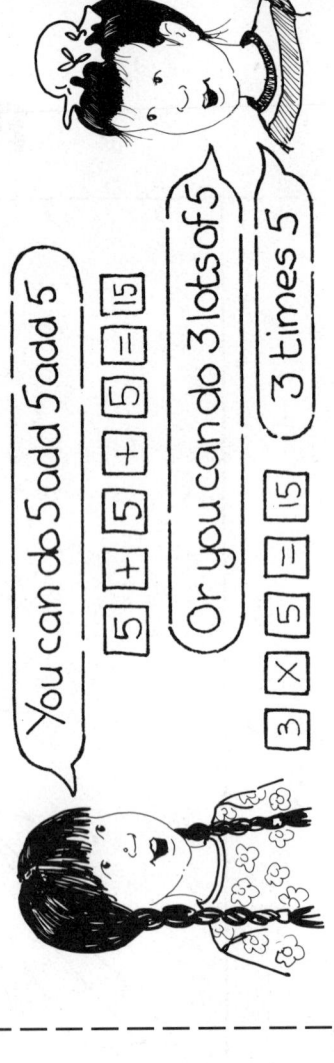

> You can do 5 add 5 add 5
> 5 + 5 + 5 = 15
> Or you can do 3 lots of 5
> 3 × 5 = 15
> 3 times 5

◆ ESSENTIALS FOR MATHS: Numbers to 20

◆ Name _____

Peanuts

◆ Colour in the peanuts. How many peanuts has each parrot got?

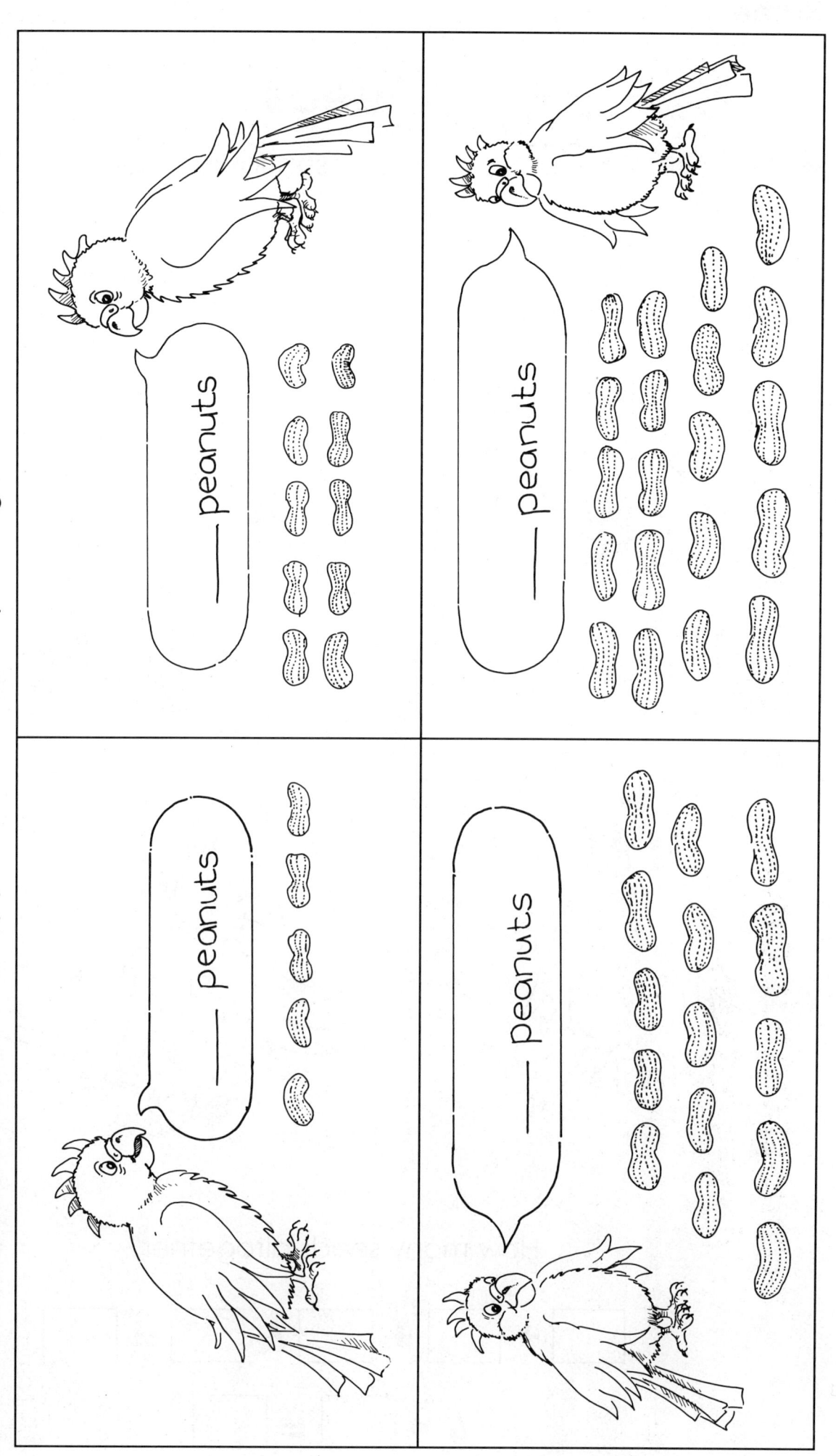

___ peanuts

___ peanuts

___ peanuts

___ peanuts

◆ ESSENTIALS FOR MATHS: Numbers to 20   19

◆ Name _____

Seeds

◆ Give each parrot _____ sunflower seeds.

How many seeds altogether?

☐ + ☐ + ☐ + ☐ = ☐

4 × ☐ = ☐

◆ ESSENTIALS FOR MATHS: Numbers to 20

◆ Name _____

Seed sums

I found 14 seeds, then I ate 4 of them.

◆ How many seeds are left? _____

◆ Check with a calculator. | 14 | − | 4 | = | |

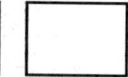

I found 20 seeds, then I ate 7 of them.

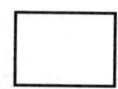

◆ How many seeds are left? _____

◆ Check with a calculator. | 20 | − | 7 | = | |

◆ Make up your own sum.

I found ___ seeds, then I ate ___ of them.

◆ How many seeds are left? _____

◆ Check with a calculator. | | − | | = | |

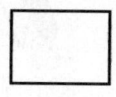

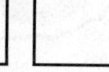

◆ ESSENTIALS FOR MATHS: Numbers to 20

Check your handwriting

Check each number in turn. Write each number three or four times on a piece of paper and look at it carefully.

◆ If you can already write a number properly, cover it over on this card with a counter. When you've checked all ten, you will see which ones you should practise.

Practise a few times each day for a week. Then check again.

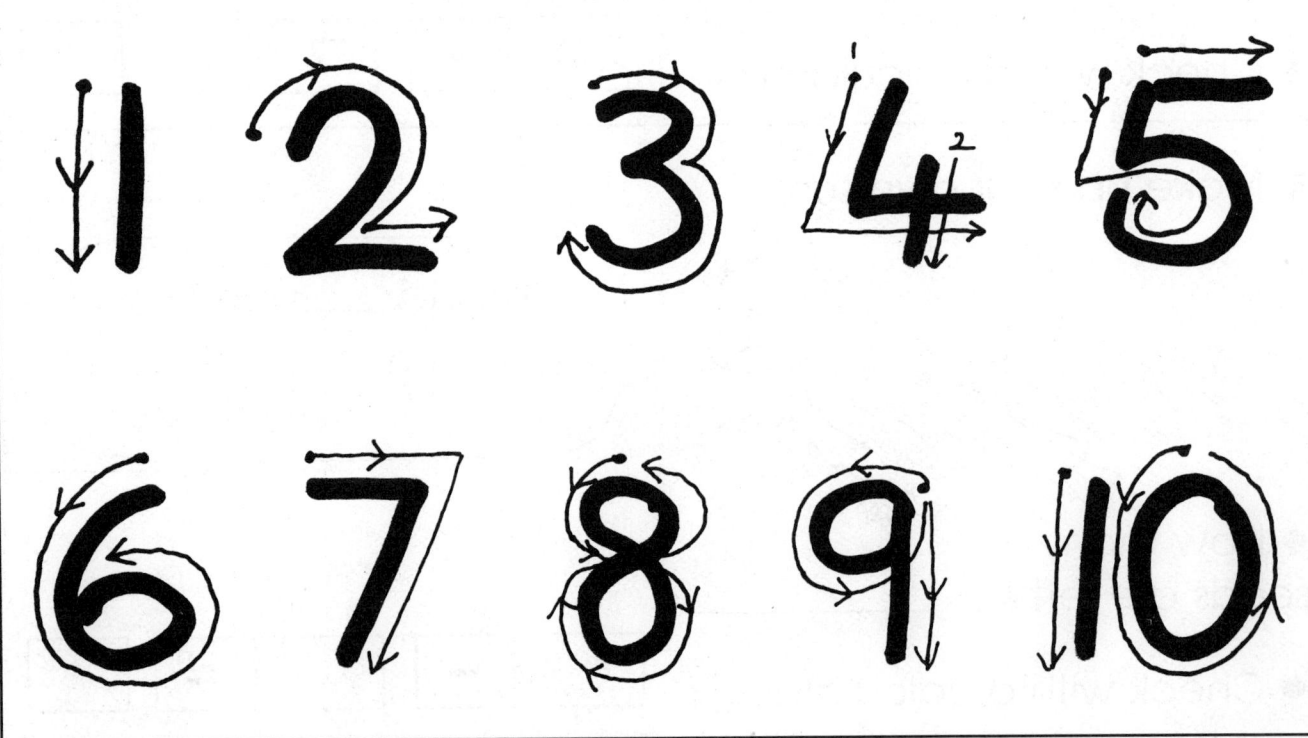

1 2 3 4 5

6 7 8 9 10

◆ ESSENTIALS FOR MATHS: Numbers to 20

◆ Name _____

Writing practice: 2s and 3s

Write ten 2s here.

Start at the top of the number.

Write ten 3s here.

Start at the top!

2 _____

2 _____

3 _____

3 _____

◆ How many things are there in each box? Write 2 or 3.

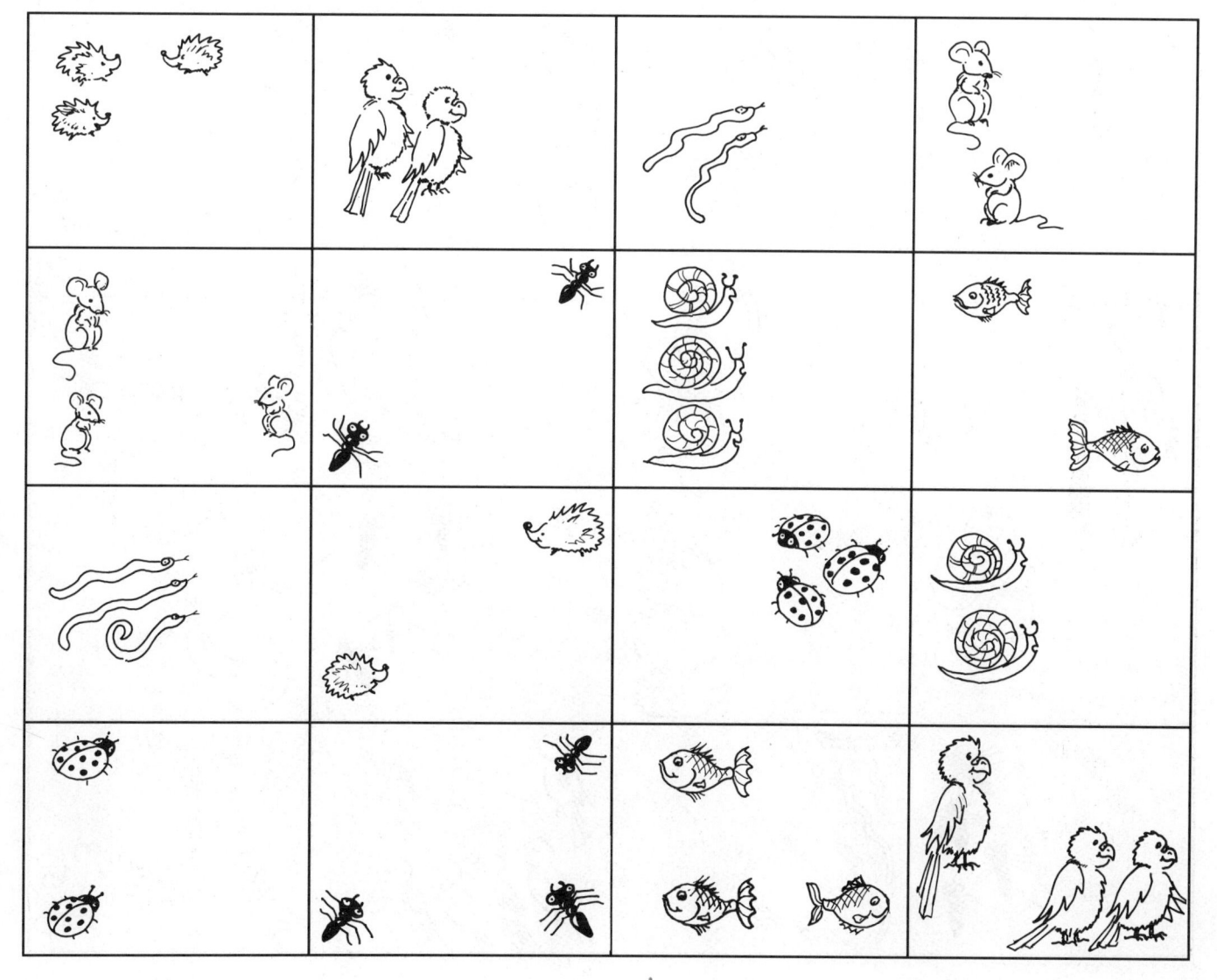

◆ ESSENTIALS FOR MATHS: Numbers to 20

23

Writing practice: 4s and 5s

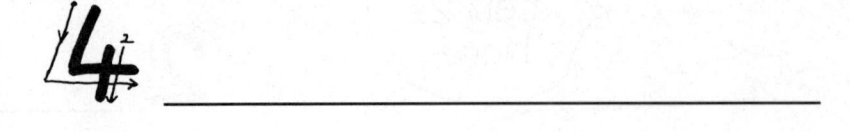

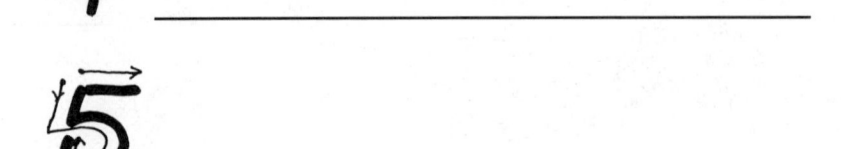

Write ten 4s here.

Remember: start at the top of the number.

4 _____

4 _____

Write ten 5s here.

Start at the top!

5 _____

5 _____

◆ How many things are there in each box? Write 4 or 5.

ESSENTIALS FOR MATHS: Numbers to 20

◆ Name _____

Writing practice: 6s, 8s and 9s

Write five 6s here.

6 6 _____

Write ten 8s here.

Start at the top!

8 _____

8 _____

Write five 9s here.

9 9 _____

◆ What number should go in each box? Write 6, 8 or 9.

◆ ESSENTIALS FOR MATHS: Numbers to 20   25

◆ Name _____

Lots of legs 1

How many legs have we got?
8 lots of 2

| 8 | X | 2 | = | |

How many legs?
4 lots of 4

| 4 | X | 4 | = | |

How many legs?
3 lots of 6

| 3 | X | 6 | = | |

How many legs?
one lot of 4

| 1 | X | 4 | = | |

How many legs?
2 lots of 8

| 2 | X | 8 | = | |

How many legs?
5 lots of none

| 5 | X | 0 | = | |

◆ ESSENTIALS FOR MATHS: Numbers to 20

26

◆ Name _____

Lots of legs 2

◆ Make up your own puzzles.
◆ Draw some more animals in each box.

Box 1 (duck):
How many legs?
___ lots of ___
□ × □ = □

Box 2 (hedgehog):
How many legs?
___ lots of ___
□ × □ = □

Box 3 (ant):
How many legs?
___ lots of ___
□ × □ = □

Box 4 (fish):
How many legs?
___ lots of ___
□ × □ = □

◆ ESSENTIALS FOR MATHS: Numbers to 20

Name _____

Caterpillars

"I've got 17 caterpillars in my tank. Sometimes, some of them escape."

"There are 6 caterpillars on me."

"and 11 in the tank."

Have any caterpillars escaped?

"There are ___ caterpillars on me."

"and ___ in the tank."

Have any caterpillars escaped?

"There are ___ caterpillars on me."

"and ___ in the tank."

Have any caterpillars escaped?

ESSENTIALS FOR MATHS: Numbers to 20

◆ Name _____

Frogs

◆ Colour in the frogs.
◆ Fold up in line with arrows, over and over, in order.

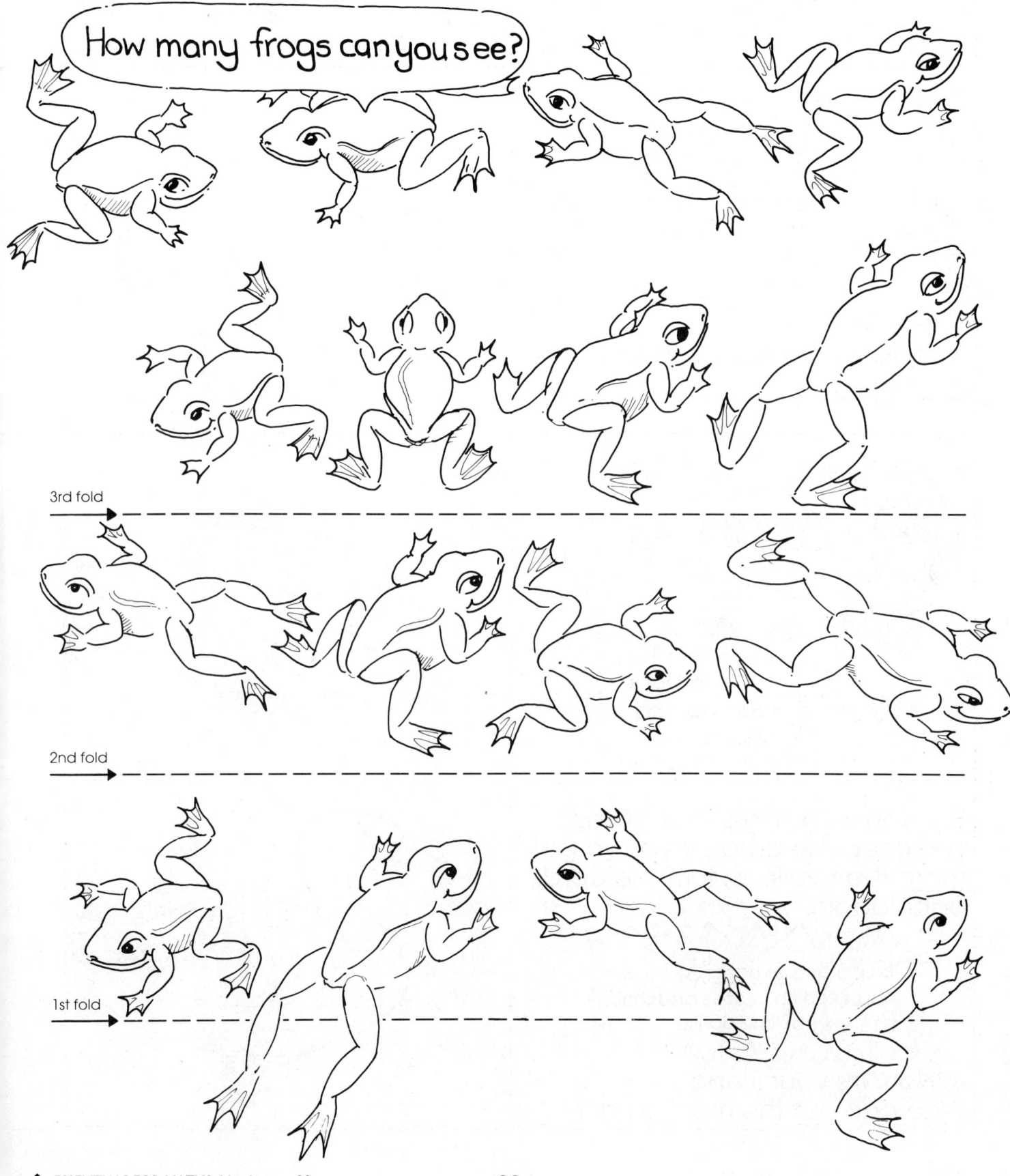

___

How many frogs can you see?

3rd fold → -

2nd fold → -

1st fold → -

◆ ESSENTIALS FOR MATHS: Numbers to 20

Legs to twenty

How to play:

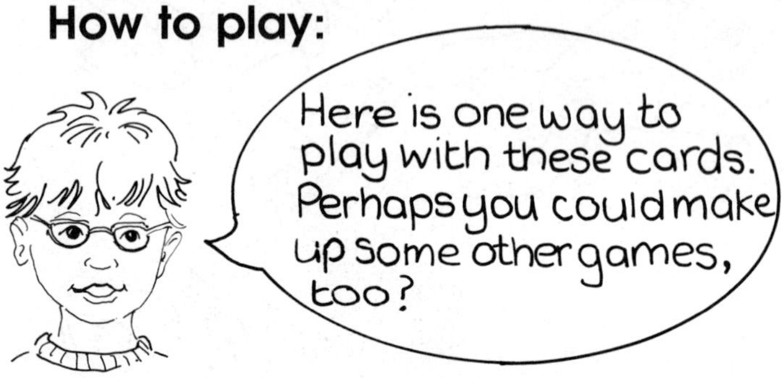

Here is one way to play with these cards. Perhaps you could make up some other games, too?

1. Shuffle the cards. Spread them all out separately, face down.

2. Turn over any four cards.

How many legs have you got?

I've got none, four, four and six... that's 14!

3. If you've got <u>less</u> than 20 legs, you keep the cards. If you've got <u>more</u> than 20 legs, turn the cards back again.

If you get <u>exactly</u> 20 legs you keep the cards and that's the end of the game.

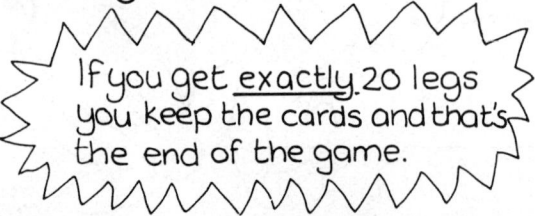

4. Now it's your friend's turn. Who can get the most cards?

◆ ESSENTIALS FOR MATHS: Numbers to 20

ESSENTIALS FOR MATHS: Numbers to 20

31

ESSENTIALS FOR MATHS: Numbers to 20

32